THE DIVINING POOL

THE DIVINING POOL

Amanda Merritt

WUNDOR

Editions

First published in Great Britain in 2017 by Wundor Editions

Wundor Editions Ltd, 35B Fitzjohn's Avenue, London NW3 5JY

www.wundoreditions.com

Book Design – Matthew Smith

ISBN 978-0-9956541-6-7

Printed and bound in Great Britain by TJ International Ltd

I would like to thank the editors of Aesthetica, Descant, Grain, Prairie Fire, Stand, and Untethered where versions of some of these poems first appeared. Thank you to Matthew Smith, Don Paterson, John Burnside, Robert Crawford, Tim Lilburn, Carla Funk, Maureen Bradley and Steven Price for their commitment to the development of my work. In many ways The Divining Pool would not exist were it not for the support of my friends and editors, specifically: Owain Nicholson, Patrick Errington, Adri Smith, Leslie Scott, Isaac Nowell, Helen Nicholson, Anna Moore, Caitlin Flynn, Liz Snell, Wendy Orr, Julie Bartusek, Tom Minogue, Tara Lawrence, and Julie Yau. Their feedback has been instrumental in the crafting of these poems. A special thanks is owed to Matthew Manera for his unwavering belief in my writing, his wisdom and his guidance. To my partner, Adrian Myszka, for keeping the torch lit along the final stretch. Most importantly, I would like to thank my mother, grandmother and aunt for the grit and ferocity of their faith in me. They have shaped me as a human being and as a writer, irrevocably.

For my family

'In the night shall I become the universe?'

Thomas the Obscure
– Maurice Blanchot

A Cure for Anxiety

Begin here:

take a sharp, heavy object
and drum it against your sternum.
Repeat until you feel the break,
chest cavity burst like bull kelp. Reach in,
hook your middle fingers round your ribs,
yard them aside like a mollusk hinge. Be swift,
because you are always half-open anyway and you
are here to finish it. Trail one finger along the heart's
left ventricle. Beneath, you should find an apple seed.
If it's not there, tuck your fingers beneath the diaphragm,
slide from left to right, slowly glissando across the stomach;
when you find it (notice how the atria rev) pause to trace
its shape, then extract the hard black shell. Submerge
in water
and expose
to sun. Soon it will
photosynthesise. Watch it
grow as you rinse your hands,
then prepare the surgical thread.

Love Myth

Charon dips his oar into the murk
and glides into the vanishing eye
of river, black as a bundle
of prehistoric sleep, bound
for passengers on the far shore.

Torch held high, the man
splits the night as he wades
hip-deep into the gullet
of a light-fevered cave,
crusted with dolomite;
its flame exhales near
the nape of his neck
as voices of wayfarers croon
from below, call out his name—

he holds his breath to hear.
But the hum from below
makes the silence stronger;
nothing now is window or mirror
except the shiver of his pulse
and the rippling dark.

The Canadian Pacific Railway

They are sound sleepers, I assure you.
– Henry David Thoreau

Grown over by broadcasts of canola,
the railroad pulls in the distance. Time
walks one foot-length of the track ahead.
Every four or five clicks we pass a few cedars
that cluster in the shade of telephone poles,
whose copper cables sag in the blue heat.
Warped beneath iron rails, the sun-split
cross ties will make a sound fire. As the wind
picks up, we pack our wares, then slide down
the crumbling ballast to the muddy river,
shifting loose a century's prairie-bleached bones.

Portrait of Persephone as a Girl

Hidden in switchgrass,
whistling to finches
that preen and flirt
behind broad fans of maple
she leans, twisting violets
through her hair, bursting
sealed buds of crocuses one
by one, bored on this hilltop,
with this late, hot summer,
dying for a cool place
to dip into the shade.

Paradise on the Juan de Fuca Strait

A wasp nest writhes
in the shade of a deck canopy.
Below, the man sits with his coffee
and Neruda's *Odas Elementales*,
thinking he too could grow
lemons, start his lemon tree
next to the riverbank,
make poppy seed lemon soap
for the baby.

The woman is strung in a hammock
between veranda posts: a spot
designed for her to sway.
A notepad rests on her belly,
moved by the small foot
beneath her skin. Pen
to her lip, she spots pigweed
between the slats.
Makes a note: *pull*.
Knots her fingers in the netting,
and the beam above her creaks
as the house shifts two centimetres
toward the bank. She fans
her face and sighs, red brands
on the backs of her arms.

The man takes another sip,
watches a wasp land on the inside
of the woman's swollen ankle.
At the caw of a raven they both
look up, the woman's gaze
fixes to the blue sky, admiring
how deftly the clouds change.

The Laurel

After Bernini's 'Apollo and Daphne'

Daphne bellies over the Aegean's edge,
limbs outspread, grasping
for an arc of air, savage abandon
wrought in every sinew of her leap,
yet stayed by the wind: foot lashed
to the brink of land by roots
so warped only her father
could have captured her there.

Magdalene with Smoking Flame

Georges de La Tour, 1640

The model he has chosen sits with her eyes downcast—
a young girl in Lunéville with downy body
and thick brown hair—*let out your braid.*
Obedient. He smiles, tops the port
in his glass, and angles the canvas.
Her messaline skin, the colour of a gypsy.
He licks amber drops from the lip
of his glass: she must stay.

She waits, gaze forced to the skull in her lap:
just a stone, a sea-washed stone porous from—*what are you thinking?*
Her eyes lock onto his like a bur on a bay-hound's coat. *Beautiful. Stay.*
He steps out from behind his canvas.　　*No, look here girl.* Her fingers unlace
from the candle on the desk, thumbprint translucent
on its edge.　　　　　Who are you painting?
He stops.　　　I mean—*You are the Magdalene.*
Cast free of the seven powers of wrath—yes look that way
toward the candle. She pauses.　　　He combs her hair
to her spine.　　　Shadows shiver out of the floorboards
as the flame blinks.　　　　　For a painter, his hands are thick.
He drapes a strand of hair across her breast.
Like the men in camp who snap buzzard necks.
She feels the uneven wood on her soles.　　Will this be done in grisaille?
He drags the candle closer, examines the contour of her brow.
No. With brush end he lifts her chin,
one eye purple in his shadow. *Never*
question a painter's method.　　She breathes in the stink
of him: linseed oil in his fingernails, cheap tobacco
on his breath. Brush tip at jaw bone now, light
hot on her eyelids, one palm tender on the skull's crown.

A Song for Lilith

Bone of my bones
and flesh of my flesh.
– Genesis 2:18-24

In the dew of an apple tree,
Adam is woken. His hands, wet,
slip confused across his chest,
catch the hilt of a blade
beneath his skin.

               Time seizes,
glides like bricks of ice
as Eve extracts her knife,
prunes a rib from its cage.

In the light of the moon
he mistakes her unflinching eyes
for stars, then she rests him
against the tree, climbs back
onto its fruit-weary bough.

The sun fans open to bird song
as she cleans the bone with her blade,
whittles holes and a mouth piece, plays.

Missing Persons

On January fifth, at 1:26 AM
in the Montrose waiting room
a woman in a green coat
carrying a black backpack
and a sign that read *Danger*
severed her reflection in the glass:
she triggered the automatic doors,
releasing two runaway halves
into the blank night of the railway station.

Mirror/ \Mirror

taught to smile with the eyes	sitting patient with the mirror
by willing soft roses to our cheeks,	we learn to shape our face
to speak sweet. Moderate	with foundation and blush,
in tone, in takings we are shown	how to kiss our lips to a tissue—
how to look and not look	single petal of *tempt 752*—
at eyes that linger too long	and flash a quick smile
examining the body,	of the woman we later reprove
that bid us lean closer	having forgotten to conceal
as we pin a jewel to our ear	that faint scar
like a livestock tag	at our scalp.

La Santa Muerte

In the doorway she slips off her shoes,
unbuckles shadow after shadow:
moulted skins on the back of a chair.

She no longer needs the light
to find her way down the hall. Still
he'll let the lamp burn low

at their bedside, where every night
he rests his watch. In its glow she leans
close to learn the grain of her lover's face

before she puts the flame out.
When she climbs into bed,
the only sound he makes: a sigh,

then with a kiss on the cheek
she unpins the crown from his watch,
cradles their heart, so it stops.

The Candle

The candle melts beneath a petal of fire
in the frosted window of a stone church.
Submerged in the love of itself it glows.

While eager to descend its own rope,
to measure the night's height
and breadth, for a moment

it wavers from reverie by a draft:
a traveller seeking shelter
from the snow.

An Offering for the Resurrection of a Child

I salve my palms with saffron—
lifeline ruddy, like a burn.
As I move, a loose barb
of your muslin shirt catches
on the fresh stitching. I find
my breath, then square the knife
and cutting board to counter edge.

While I work, shingles warm,
snow slides off in packs.
Fine bars of silver light
spin on drifts of dust
across the carpet:
an avian cell. Radiant
as fired steel, day burns
on its own tension, snow
redoubles the light.

I place the muscle
on the counter. Ragged
as a wing-torn bird,
its atrophied walls
falter, then seep
a small river. I extract
the knife, dust the incision
with thyme and wipe my wrist
beneath my eye;
it is tough meat tonight.

Outside, the gutter's incessant
stream of water scores the air:
soon the leaves must be cleared.

I, with my fear of ladders,
drive the knife into the septum

even deeper. Two halves now, splayed
and gutted like a fig, and my hand stops
to wonder what spell makes a heart begin.

The Watcher

Every angel is terrible.
– Rilke

A viola floats Casimir Ney
up the subway staircase. Preludes
to nothing but preludes. On the platform,
she noticed him then; not his eyes
but their darkness.

He never slept, sat up late
in the living room with his book,
half aglow, bent forward—always
making space for ghosts.

She had lived like a marble block:
his own Pietà. After his disappearance
she moved through their house
like a barking owl, like dust—
always in losing light. Strata clouds
split her frontal lobes, and arias
stung her brain like electricity on water.
Then something in her hands faltered,
cracked palms repelled by the neck
of her instrument, by one another.

Behind the sun-slant field the house waits
to be lit. A cool wind whistles the first three notes
of a minor scale. Through the dusk, she looks back,
knows the darkness crouching there.

Oh Alice,

dream me a door into the early dark
a gap through the one-way glass

I've pressed my face against
clawing for a latch

far too long

peering in at the shadows
that shift like koi in a clouded pool

that flicker and recoil
when I raise my lamp.

Brother

You clutch the crooks of your elbows,
hungry. Place your weight on the table—
head hung with rot: the wilt of summer in you.
Sweet, so sweet. A brilliance I've always envied,
never understood. I slide you my coffee
and your spine hackles. *Too dark*, you say.
Your mouth a fallen maple seed. Stained:
snuff or blood, the colour of aged brick,
a malting sun, or a strip of arbutus skin
pinned down. *Does the cosmic space
in which we dissolve taste of us?* Your tulip hands
unfurl and you smile at me.
          I would have argued—I must have.
I pour myself more coffee.
Light weathers through the window—
a bolt of hide that will not touch you,
too much the same element.
The hall clock strikes five, unwinds,
and your eyes darken, those clotted gems:
sometimes even I forget you cannot see.
Hands to your chin, your veins
are coarse chords of tobacco.
This is you in sepia, I say. *I am nauseous.*
          It'll get better, I would have said—I must have.
You turn to the window: heat
from the pines bends the sky and I feel your heart
belt the edge of the table. Then you grip
the wings of your shoulder blades
and disappear.

For the Diviner

Wrists soft-side up, I beg you:
break me. From spleen
to sternum. Spill fog from my lungs,
take your kullenschiff and split
bronchi to trachea to tongue.
Snap the pulmonary artery
from that silver cyst in my chest—
lift its small looking glass
in your wide palm and tell me
what happened in the canyons
of Tucuman, where we played
when we were children.
Bring it to your lips and breathe,
wipe your thumb across its surface,
ink it with your fingerprints
(because it is yours now),
whisper what you see—tell me
where has my brother gone.

Winter Garden

The dead are the dysrhythmia of the earth
that swoon through the blood, hiccup in the ears,
rail past the corner of the eye—make you turn,
make you turn back twice.

Closets of clothing heap them into a pile
like drifts of leaves, and spoon-carve
a cavity in the dark. Lie down, fold yourself in.
This isn't him. These are his skins.

You have drunk the evening—world blown-out,
gently spinning; yet to love the evening you must be
the corpse flower, grow from a nocturnal garden
though not even your simple heart is centre. Now
there is no need to lock the doors, draw down
the shades, shut your eyes when the night
sits gently on the edge of your bed.

During the day, winter's Zolpidem
slows the blood as rage stiffens
like an artery. Understand this:
real violence is not in devastation,
it's the sudden, terrifying seizure—

sometimes this blur at your peripheries,
like headlights through the kitchen window,
like a tune coming from nowhere in particular.
Leading away. Sometimes this is more real:
the dark casing around stars.

Aletheia

May I gaze in your mirror?
Do you always look up
from the surface of the well?
Teach me your language.
Come to me in the mud
of a November field
at the roadside with hot tea.
Bright stranger, come to me
in the street where I post
my letters, warm your hands
on my back. Signal to me
with the wrappers in the gutter.
Follow me home. Undress,
step into my warm shower,
commune with me, oh come
and sit on the edge of the tub.
Hold me like a noun,
then etch your equation
in the scum of the tiles. Kiss me
so I know just how you taste.

An Address to the God of Salvation

You: a tired, dirty old word
grey as December.
Whistling your hymns
you puff existence
from your tall brick chimney
and carry on shovelling,
blessing us each
with a kiss on the head
as we toss our coal on the fire.

How many have cued,
clasped their hands, bowed
their heads to hear a word
from you? With a twinkle
in your eye, and a nod
of your chin you send us
curious into the other room.

But you are no doctrine, no need.
Common as quartz
beneath the soil, you teach
existence through staggering
existence because time holds you—
self-made martyr—a single
halide emulsified, splitting
and splitting the nucleus of life.
No, you will not unravel back
to your source, emerge a negative
from the warm acetic water.

Cliff Jumping

Like the myoclonic jolt
which wakes you, seconds
before hitting water, roadway
or ice, is it the shock
that prepares your muscles
for the fall, recalls
your essence from the air
like a diver, surfacing?

Stepping off—
a sudden absence
beneath the feet
and your last breath
as practiced as a dreamer's:
a ripple after the surface breaks.

Fever

The doors are blocked with ice.
At the centre of the room, a man,
bones slicked by beads of light,
hunches before the belly of the stove.
Its fire can't thaw his thick marrow,
or the silence that frosts the empty cabin.

Wool squeals into ash and the question
of being flares from the open oven
as he folds coals into his clothes,
listening for footfall through
pleats of tumbling snow.

Through the window,
where the wood stack
is packed under:
a white timberline,
the white pines.

On Not Finding Him

After Li Po

The sound of barking runs
across the pearl-grey water
where peach blossoms nod,
heavy with rain. It must be noon,
but I cannot hear the bells,
only the breath of deer
who weave, curious,
between screens of Silver Pines.
At this distance nothing moves
on the jade peak ahead:
waterfalls hang like painted scrolls.
I lean against the nearest tree,
stopped by the stream.
No man will find him here.

Spring

The still lifes of spiders glitter,
strung along the ceiling, laced
between toy boughs of bonsai,
swinging from the Iranian rug—
each web copper in the bloodshot
eye of the sun. Their watching worlds
swell with every wall's sigh.
As the phantoms wake, roused
by Earth's new anxieties, and rove
between rooms, they brandish
their ring of keys, opening windows,
blinking at the light.

The Visitor

I take one step out of bed
and the floorboard snaps
like a glass decanter.
Then the bathroom door swings
open at the end of the foyer
and the light flicks quickly off.

As the shadow moves
I catch a hint of perfume
and her doused cigarette.
I freeze. The moon, rising
wide-eyed in the window
above, silhouettes her robe
as she exhales, slowly
adjusting to the dark.

Who's there? She asks.
The house holds its breath
as she turns back to the mirror—
waist cinched, sleeve spread
open over a cocked hip—
other hand in her curlers,
chiding: *Go back to bed.*
Mom needs a little more time
to remember her face.

Paper Lantern

Our wish rises, past the sparks
of early stars as its teardrop shadow
sails across the clock tower's face
and drifts away from the city.

Below, constellations flicker on,
lamp by lamp, as night gathers
at the ocean's seam. Its flame
swells from a brush with the west-
running wind, wavers once,
then dives for the sea.

Avatar Grove, BC

Camera at your hip
and curved spines
of hemlock in hand,
we scaled the shoulder
of rainforest. In the halo
of a tipped, big leaf maple
we stripped each other down,
braced against the horns
of the levelled tree, churning
the colours of the leaves
with our feet: ankles wet
in that understory
where your camera,
forgotten beneath the blades
of fern, cached a day
for which we never returned.

The Tide

Over the escarpment, below
white waves of the Atlantic,
giants sleep. Motionless
in the sand, their barnacled
crowns sink into sea where,
dying for home, they fell.

Their children walk ahead,
past one blurred figure
who has stopped, body
still visible on the skyline.

Suddenly the sow thistles
on this crag are taller
than we are, and the light
is nearly gone. As we walk,
the steps of the coastal path
dissolve, like a rug underfoot
the horizon slips;

we have lost sight of the others.
Water slithers through the reeds,
silencing the grasshoppers. Everywhere
the vacant field ripples purple, gold.

The Waterfall Effect

A summer breeze cools
the runoff between my breasts,

soft as the cotton
of this balled-up dress.

Lit over the river
by the lowering sun,

the rock face
becomes a god.

In its shadow, you sit
on a knuckle of stone,

scaled with spray.
I call and all you hear

is the voice of white water.
I look back, the land rushes away.

A Philosophical Meditation on the Impossibility of Contact

I wanted to write you. But these glyphs fall
straight through the lines of the page,
get stuck waist-deep at the margins, skittering counter-
crosswise and clockways and you'd hate them,
eventually. They cannot be saved.
Well, I hate the human predicament,
but that's not original. What if
the hum of the refrigerator is slowly changing
the frequency of our brains? There, I see it.
The look on your face—left eyebrow raised,
a dimple in each cheek. Smile at me.
You shake your head and the light quivers
in your eye. You smile anyway. The extra-white tip
of your canine tooth. If you were here I'd finally
teach you how to foxtrot, build you a fire and read you
my poetry. I'd quit making you mad. Don't be mad;
it doesn't matter now, that's why. Now it is time to wait.

Sometimes the length of a moment is too agonising,
so we bloodlet time from the softest places:
our thighs, and ankles and baby toes, then stare at it,
useless in a puddle on the floor. Looking forward
is nothing to celebrate. I am not looking forward to my return,
to the scent of your skin on my sheets. As all day
the heron on its stilt watches for a single fish,
I wait: tense for the soul to leap clear of its element.

I wanted to send you this letter. But through a layer
of sealed saliva, piles of thumbprints, and 8,160 miles
we'd touch, presto: contact. So I've left
to callous my fingertips with the texture of the earth
before I am tucked into it. To be in doubt
and be okay with it, where doubt finds its wellspring

in the body. And to be is to fill each capillary, each blood cell
with the knowledge of the heron and the fish and the tide pool at sundown.
Let me know if you'd like to mop up a little time.
I'm sorry darling.
When I've arrived, I'll send you a letter.

North Sea

Oh the mad coupling of hope and effort
In which we merged and despaired.
– Pablo Neruda

Each wave is the shape
of its desire, each
balanced on its break—
the crest and curve,
strain and release
of the moon's abiding
love for the earth.

The Mean Time

To eat a twenty-minute meal,
empty the Malbec as we empty
the mind, undress, touch
and have sex, slip
into a warm bed, separate
dreams. Share a cafetière
at eleven, kiss in the doorway
and hand over love
like a borrowed key.
Agree on the average,
middle, mean, be half
what the other half needs,
then pitch our bottles
over the break of day,
soak up the horizon's slow
leak from a hill beyond town.

The Pier, Howe Sound

After Li Bai

Stripped of day's rimy film,
the moon steps from the wreath
of her robe and bares heaven's scars—
deep as the bay of your departure.

Spring wind, awake in the poplars,
shakes silver coins from the boughs:
their aerial dive evening's only sound.
Above you, a knot of catkins swing,
which I pick and turn over in my hands.

You smile—moon adrift on still water,
stern of scow in hand—and take
their young green heart as an offer.

At the Window

After Paul Éluard

Sky, I have outlasted you, shed
your dew-lined coat in a pool of night.
Whole plains lay open in my hands:

inert horizons doubled, indifferent.
Brow against the glass, through the fog
of my waiting I sketch her figure on the pane,

watch it appear and expire as dawn
drains the city streets of ink and draws,
somewhere, nearer her window.

Departure

The body of water
                    shifts
                              breathes slow as sleep

                                                  To the west
                              mist collects like down
     in the crevices between
                              low-lying mountains
Cumulus waves
                    weep at the shoreline of the gulf

                                        dense with refracted light

          At 600 feet   the coast shimmers with sundown

               elevated like a fingerprint   lifted

     from the page of a book   pulse

          impalpable

                                   across the expanse   of a sheet
drawn lightly
               over the shape of the land

Little Warrior

For CF

A cloudless autumn blue
has taken no inspiring shapes
today, though the palette
resembles a dream—pink cuticle
of Abraham Darby, the cheeks
of a six-year-old girl, reaching
from her father's shoulders
for the window of a castle ruin.

A Spot of Time

In the lavender field the children hide,
counting out thousands beneath their breath.
Watchful and curious about the work of bees
they duck and follow: sun hats on drawstrings
swinging at their backs lift as white puppets
to the breeze, revealing all their magic places.

They play until their loose hair fills with gold
and shadows fold into the long stalks of lavender.
At the call of the dinner bell, they burst
like gophers from the ground, then wave
their purple wands and whistle as they fly
down the field with the warblers in the sycamore trees.

The Argentine Tango

The dancers take their mark
on a makeshift Teatro
to the silence of the street,
air dense with ripened peach:
the sweat of this Buenos Aires
evening. The people have stopped,
stand with bundles of cloth
and baskets of grapes, poised
to watch. With a twist of the arm
the barrel organ begins, whistles
La Cumparsita through its teeth,
music draws round the dancers:
hemmed to earth by the heat. *Apilado,*
he cries, and they restack their bones,
enfold like the wings of a whispering
heron on the bank of the River Silver.
Salida, energy of earth
charges the feet, dust sparking
off dock palette planks, *barrida,*
hardwood flexing as thighs meet,
sole to knee, *caricias,* slum waters
braided beneath. He steps forward,
caminata, lamp-lit alley tense
with the heat of attention
as she spins, *ocho ocho,* and they lean
into the buoyant space between bodies:
a small resistance, twin poles
bound by their parting embrace.

Dear,

if I knew the exact measure,
I would calculate the dimension
of the universe and subtract your shadow,
the sylph who steps behind, at last to know
the slant of your shoulders against the hill;
the tilt of your hips
as you rise,
seeking shade
among the maples.